Tragedy in London

PLAGUE and FIRE

Contents

London – a dangerous place to live   2

Danger in the docks   6

The first deaths   8

Killing the cats and dogs   10

Finding a cure   12

Burying the dead   14

London tinderbox   16

The flames take hold   18

Fighting the fire   20

The city destroyed   22

Rebuilding London   24

A safer London   26

Glossary   28

Index   29

Disaster in London   30

Written by Richard Platt   Illustrated by Barbara Gibson

London – a dangerous place to live

England's greatest city was a foul place to live in 1665. The streets were dirty, and stank. Rats ran everywhere, and fed on rubbish. Even the air and the water weren't clean. Coal fires turned the sky grey. Filth from drains **polluted** streams and London's great river, the Thames.

For the city's poor people, life was very hard. They were often hungry. Their homes were dark, damp **slums** and two or even three families lived in homes built for one. It wasn't easy to get enough **fuel** to keep warm.

Ships and boats filled the River Thames in 1665.

London looked very different from today. There were few large buildings. The narrow streets were dusty in summer and muddy in winter. Along them were many small wooden houses, which were very close together and often badly built and falling down. For a traveller, the easiest way through the city was on the river and ferry-boats zipped along it and across it.

Altogether there were about 400,000 people living in London in the spring of 1665. No British city was bigger. London's huge size, though, could not protect its people. Londoners were about to face two frightening and deadly dangers which threatened rich and poor alike.

London's poor did not live very long – half of them died before their sixth birthday. The other half were lucky to live 40 years. If they were unlucky, illness killed them sooner.

About 300 years earlier a terrible disease had struck London. It was called the plague, or the Black Death.

The awful signs were easy to spot. Those who caught the plague suffered a high **fever**. Some were confused; they had headaches and backache. Soon smooth blisters, called buboes, swelled at the tops of their legs, on their necks or under their arms. Days later most died a painful death.

The Black Death killed about a third of all Britons. In London 200,000 people may have died. Since then the plague returned from time to time, when the weather was hot. Londoners knew that each summer more people might die, but nobody knew why.

London's poor were particularly at risk in 1665. There had been a **drought** the year before, and the lack of rain meant food plants died in the dry fields. Many families went hungry. An icy winter weakened them further – people did not have money to buy fuel to keep themselves warm. When the plague returned to London in 1665 they did not have the strength to fight it.

Many poor people died from the plague.

5

Danger in the docks

The plague that hit London in the spring of 1665 came from Holland. The River Thames was London's link to the world. In riverside **docks** hundreds of sailing ships unloaded. They brought valuable goods, such as timber, fine cloth and china crockery from ports in Europe and beyond. But they also brought the disease with them.

Londoners knew that the plague was killing thousands of people in Holland and they thought **Dutch** crews might be ill with the disease. To stop the plague reaching England again, Dutch ships had to wait for 40 days at Canvey, an island downriver. If anyone on board died, the ship could not sail on to London.

Ships that were allowed to enter London's docks tied up at the **wharves** that lined the river. As the sailors came ashore, unwelcome passengers scurried down the ship's ropes: rats.

Londoners feared that the Dutch sailors would spread the plague, but they were wrong. The rats were the real danger. Fleas in the rats' fur carried the disease. Flea bites made the rats ill and when the rats died, the fleas jumped on to humans, and bit them.

The first deaths

In 1665, poor people who lived near the docks got the plague first. In their crowded homes, fleas hopped easily from one person to another, spreading the disease quickly through families.

Poor victims did not matter much to London's officials, so they did not record the names of the first people who died of the plague.

Houses were built close together and lots of people lived in each one.

Mary Porteous was the first victim whose name
we know. She was buried on 12 April 1665. By the end
of May, ten more people had died. As spring
became summer, the disease spread even quicker.
Each part of London had to keep death records
which showed how many died each week in
the **neighbourhood**. In one week in September,
the records showed that 8,297 Londoners had died and
7,165 of those were plague victims.

burying plague victims outside London

9

Killing the cats and dogs

Fear spread faster than the disease itself. On the doors of houses where people died, officials chalked a red cross. This sign warned everyone to stay away. Soon they did more. If one member of a family caught the plague London's rulers ordered the house doors to be locked shut. Guards standing outside made sure no one with the disease got out of their houses. Plague sufferers and their families were prisoners in their homes. People believed this would stop the disease passing from the sick to the healthy. However, they didn't know that it was the fleas that spread the disease. Locked doors could not keep out fleas or even rats. The plague continued to spread.

Men guarded houses where plague victims were living.

The rats that spread the plague travelled widely throughout London.

Londoners thought the causes of the plague were bad
smells, bad food, bad water … and pets! Fearing that
cats and dogs spread the disease, London's mayor
ordered them to be killed. Thousands of cats and dogs
were destroyed, but it didn't stop the plague. In fact,
killing pets may have even made things worse. With no
cats and dogs to kill the rats, there were more rats
in London.

Finding a cure

The summer of 1665 was one of
the hottest anyone could remember.
As London baked in the heat, more
people died. Wealthy families **fled**
the city in panic. They went to their
country houses, where they felt safe.
In July 1665 the king, Charles II, left
London and fled to Salisbury, 130
kilometres away.

Charles II

London, once a busy city, changed completely.
Tradesmen closed their shops, and people stayed inside
their homes to avoid the plague. London was quiet.
Those who had to stay searched for **cures**.
Doctors gave out treacle and walnuts, herbs
and salt, which they thought would stop
people getting the disease. They also
told people to wear a lucky charm
around their necks. But without
modern drugs or knowledge, doctors
could do nothing.

a lucky charm

Special plague doctors looked at sick people to decide
if they had caught the disease. To avoid catching it
himself, a doctor would wear a long gown, a leather
hat, gloves and a mask with a beak. Herbs inside
the beak were supposed to make the air pure
and protect the doctor. The herbs didn't
work, and neither did the costly
"cures", such as
a drink containing
real gold, that
the doctors sold.
Many plague "doctors"
were cheats and had no
medical training.

One rich man who decided
to stay in London was
a writer called Samuel Pepys.
He described the plague in
a diary, where he wrote that
many people sniffed and chewed
tobacco, believing its strong
smell would protect them.
But that didn't work either.

Burying the dead

Each week, there were more red crosses on doors. When the plague first struck, families dug graves with care. They buried their dead in coffins. But as more died, grave-diggers made huge open graves, called plague pits, in churchyards. They piled in bodies side by side. Vicars who usually buried three people a week were holding 450 **hasty** funerals each week.

Carts toured the streets collecting the dead. Those pushing them rang bells to warn away the healthy. But so many died that the endless ringing scared the living so then the carts patrolled in silence.

When autumn came, the disease began to weaken. Cool weather killed the fleas that spread the disease. In November just 4,000 died of the plague, compared with 26,000 in September. The streets of London began to fill with people again. Families returned to their homes. Tradesmen opened their shops once more. King Charles II returned to London at the end of 1665, by which time the plague had killed 100,000 Londoners.

London tinderbox

By the summer of 1666 there were very few cases of the plague in London, but there was another danger – fire. Most homes were built of wood and they had roofs of straw, reeds or thin wooden tiles called shingles. Householders kept out the rain by painting the walls with **tar**. All of these materials burnt easily.

Narrow streets helped to spread fires. The tall houses were wider at the roof than at ground level. The top floors of opposite houses almost touched.

There were many houses and shops on London Bridge.

Houses and shops even crowded the road across London's only river bridge. Fire had already destroyed the bridge twice, in 1212 and again in 1633, killing 43 people.

At a bread shop in Pudding Lane, a baker went to bed. First, though, he stacked firewood next to his warm oven to dry out. By morning, the sticks would catch fire easily to heat his oven. Perhaps too easily. Some time after midnight on Sunday, 2 September 1666 he awoke. There was a smell of smoke and the sound of crackling flames.

The flames take hold

FIRE! The bakery was in flames! The baker and his family ran from their burning home across their neighbours' roof. Only their servant – a young maid – stayed behind, because she was scared of heights.

Not far away, London's mayor gazed at the blaze from his window. He was not worried. Fires were **common**. "Pish …" the mayor said, "… a woman could put it out!" and he went back to bed.

But no one could put out the fire. A strong wind spread the flames. They crackled from the bakery and licked at the houses around it. Because the houses were so close together it was easy for the flames to leap from one building to another. At the end of the street a warehouse storing fuel and tar burned fiercely. Soon everyone had woken. Some **fled** quickly, taking only their most prized **possessions**.

Fighting the fire

Many Londoners stayed near their homes and tried to fight off the flames. They threw on water drawn from London's river. To fetch it, neighbours formed long lines. They filled leather buckets and passed them from hand to hand. Even the king helped carry water. There were a few small hand-pumps, but they squirted feeble jets.

Water could not put out the flames, so people began pulling down houses. They aimed to make gaps between the buildings that the flames could not cross. First they used hooks on long poles. When this didn't work, sailors tried using gunpowder to destroy houses. This failed, too. The fire was so hot that it burnt the **rubble** in the streets.

The city destroyed

By Monday, 3 September, flames were licking at
the city's churches. They were the last to burn because
they were made of stone as well as wood. Their lead
roofs melted. Bells fell clanging from their steeples.
The fire raged on for a third night, but the morning
finally brought relief. The wind that had been fanning
the flames dropped and the fire soon died.

Londoners picked their way through the ashes where
their homes had once stood. Two-thirds of the city –
13,200 houses – had burnt to the ground. To everyone's
amazement, just six people had died. One of them was
the maid who was too scared to escape from
the baker's shop where the fire started.

Rebuilding London

To a few people, the fire was not a disaster.
It was a chance to create a new, better city.
Even before the ashes were cold, **architects**
were designing a great new London.
The fire had destroyed crowded,
winding lanes. In their place they
planned wide streets and open squares.

However, Londoners did not want
a grand new city. They wanted their
old city back. By spring 1667 workers
had cleared the ashes and rubble.

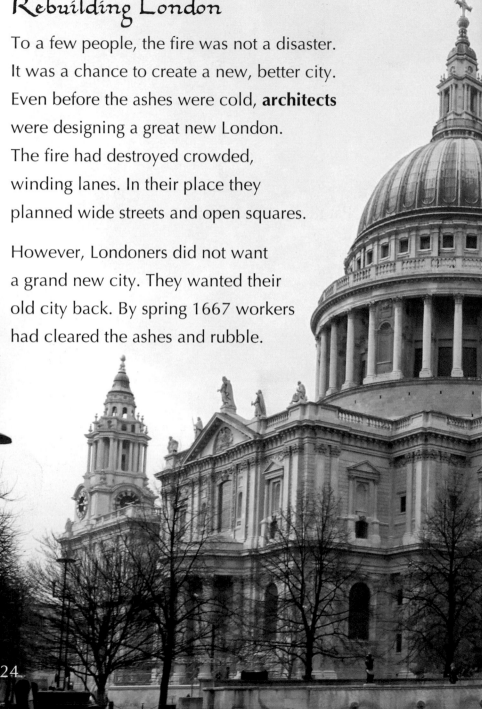

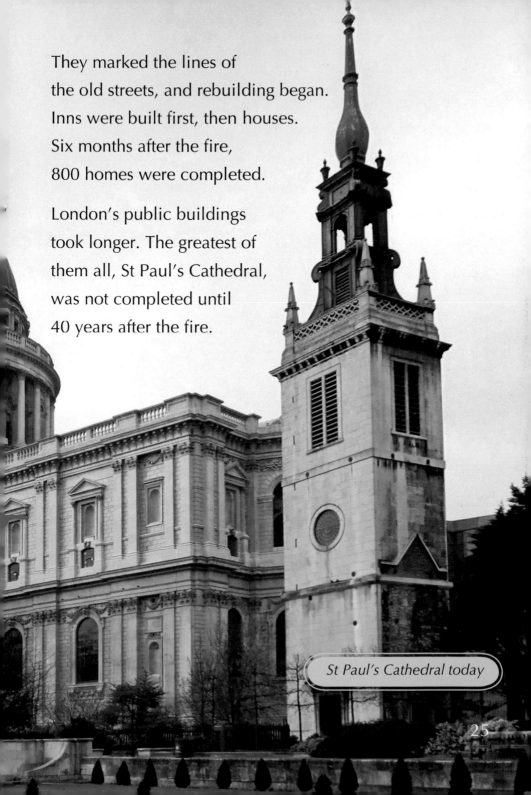

They marked the lines of
the old streets, and rebuilding began.
Inns were built first, then houses.
Six months after the fire,
800 homes were completed.

London's public buildings
took longer. The greatest of
them all, St Paul's Cathedral,
was not completed until
40 years after the fire.

St Paul's Cathedral today

A safer London

Was the new London better than the old one? It was definitely safer. New laws made sure of that. Building rules **banned thatch** and wood so houses were rebuilt using brick and stone. Walls and roofs had to be **fireproof**. The Great Fire of London of 1666 would never happen again.

But the crowded slums returned as the city was rebuilt. Dirty, hungry people returned to the slums. The rats returned too, but not the plague. It wasn't until 300 years later that doctors realised that rats had spread the plague, but no one knows why it never returned to kill as many Londoners as it did in 1665.

Despite its tragic past, London is now a big, lively city, where nearly eight million people live and work.

Glossary

architects people who design buildings

banned did not allow

common happening often

cures things you can do to stop an illness or disease

docks places where ships are tied up and unloaded

drought a time when there isn't much rain

Dutch coming from Holland

fever an illness which gives someone a very high temperature

fireproof unable to catch fire

fled escaped or ran away from

fuel something you can burn, like wood, to keep warm, to cook or to light your home

hasty hurried

neighbourhood an area in a town or city which has its own name

polluted spoilt something by adding bad things to it

possessions the things someone owns

rubble broken building materials like brick or stone

slums places with badly-built houses, where poor people live

tar a sticky black paste used for waterproofing

thatch a roof covering made from dry reeds

tradesmen people who run their own businesses, doing jobs for others or selling things

wharves a place built next to water, where ships can be unloaded

Index

architects   24

Black Death   4, 5

buboes   4

churches   22

cures   12, 13

deaths from fire   16, 23

deaths from plague   5, 8, 9, 15

docks   6, 7, 8

fever   4

fire   2, 16, 17, 18, 19, 20, 21,
22, 23, 24, 25, 26

fleas   7, 8, 10, 15

graves   14

gunpowder   21

houses   3, 10, 12, 16, 19, 21,
23, 25, 26

King Charles II   12, 15

mayor of London   11, 18

plague   4, 5, 6, 7, 8, 9, 10, 11,
12, 13, 14, 15, 16, 27

plague doctors   13

plague pits   14

poor people   2, 3, 4, 5, 8

Pudding Lane   17

rats   2, 7, 10, 11, 27

red cross   10, 14

river   2, 3, 6, 7, 16, 20

Samuel Pepys   13

slums   2, 27

St Paul's Cathedral   25

streets   2, 3, 14, 15, 16, 21, 24,
25

water   2, 11, 20, 21

Plague

Fleas on the rats spread the plague.

People caught the plague.

Doctors wore special masks.

Survivors buried the dead in plague pits.

Guards stood outside plague houses.

The plague killed 100,000 people in London.

Fire

A baker's shop caught fire.

The fire spread from one house to another.

Sailors blew up houses to stop the fire spreading.

Londoners fetched water from the Thames.

Only six people died in the fire, but 13,200 houses were destroyed.

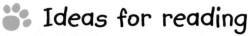

Ideas for reading

Written by Clare Dowdall, Phd
Lecturer and Primary Literary Consultant

Learning objectives: read independently and with increasing fluency longer and less familiar texts; read less common alternative graphemes including trigraphs; draw together ideas and information from across a whole text; give some reasons why things happen; explain ideas and processes using imaginative and adventurous vocabulary and non-verbal gestures to support communication

Curriculum links: History: What do we know about the Great Fire of London?

Interest words: plague, architects, banned, cures, docks, drought, Dutch, fever, fireproof, fled, fuel, hasty, neighbourhood, polluted, possessions, rubble, slums, tar, thatch, tradesmen, wharves

Word count: 2,101

Resources: paper and pens

Getting started

- Ask if any children have visited the city of London, and what it is like. Explain that they will be reading about what London was like nearly 400 years ago.

- Read the title with children and describe what the plague was. Look carefully at the words *Plague and Fire* to notice one letter that is pronounced differently. Introduce the trigraph *gue* and distinguish it from the grapheme *g*. Show children some examples, e.g. stage, rage, wage/vague, plague.

- Explain that this is an information book and that it describes two true events: the plague and the Great Fire of London. Ask children to read the blurb silently and recount the information to a partner.

Reading and responding

- Turn to pp2–3. Read this aloud with the children. Check that children understand how London in 1665 was different from today.

- Based on reading pp2–3, help children to practise retrieving information about the city and make deductions by asking questions, e.g. *Why was it easiest for travellers to travel on the river?*